The
goat monster
and other stories

Nelson

Thomas Nelson and Sons Ltd
Nelson House   Mayfield Road
Walton-on-Thames   Surrey
KT12 5PL   UK

51 York Place
Edinburgh
EH1 3JD   UK

Thomas Nelson (Hong Kong) Ltd
Toppan Building 10/F
22A Westlands Road
Quarry Bay   Hong Kong

Thomas Nelson Australia
102 Dodds Street
South Melbourne
Victoria 3205   Australia

Nelson Canada
1120 Birchmount Road
Scarborough Ontario
M1K 5G4   Canada

© Macmillan Education Ltd 1987
This edition © Thomas Nelson & Sons Ltd 1992
Editorial Consultant: Donna Bailey
Written by Ron Deadman
'The goat monster' was illustrated by Sue Lisansky
'The wicked tiger' was illustrated by Sara Silcock
'The fox in the water' was illustrated by Steve Smallman

First published by Macmillan Education Ltd 1987
ISBN 0-333-41891-3

This edition published by Thomas Nelson and Sons Ltd 1992

ISBN 0-17-400616-0
NPN 9 8 7 6 5 4

Printed in Hong Kong

The goat monster

Once upon a time there was a little goat
who lived with his mother in a cave
on the hillside.
Sometimes he asked his mother if he could go
outside the cave to play, but his mother
would not let him.

"You are too small," she said. "The tiger or
the jackal will catch you and eat you up."
So little goat stayed in the cave.

Every day the little goat grew a little bigger.
One day he said to himself, "I am big enough
to go out of the cave now."
 So when his mother was not looking,
he left the cave and went for a walk.
He saw a cow eating grass near the cave.
 "What a big, strong goat!" he said to himself.
He had never seen any other animals, so
he did not know it was a cow.

"Hello," he said to the cow. "How did you grow so big and strong?"

"I eat grass every day," said the cow.

"My mother eats grass too," said the little goat, "but she isn't as big and strong as you."

"That is because I eat better grass," said the cow. "I eat the rich green grass in the forest."

Now the little goat wanted to be big and strong too, so he said to the cow, "Please will you show me where this rich green grass is."

"Come with me," said the cow.

So the cow took the little goat into the forest.
It was dark inside the forest and
the little goat was afraid, but
the grass was thick and rich and green.
The little goat ate so much grass that
his tummy was quite full.

Then the cow said, "It is time to
go home now," but the little goat's tummy
was so full that he couldn't move.

"You go," he said to the cow.
"I'll go home tomorrow."

The little goat looked for a place to stay
for the night.
He found a big hole in the ground.
"This will do nicely," he said to himself and
he got into the hole in the ground.
But the little goat didn't know that
the hole was the home of a jackal.
The jackal was out that day visiting
his friend the tiger.

Later that night when it was nearly dark,
the jackal came back to his hole in the ground.
He tried to go inside but he couldn't get in
and he woke up the little goat, who
opened his eyes wide.
All the jackal could see in the hole was
a pair of big shining eyes.
The jackal was very afraid.

"Oh dear, oh dear!" said the jackal.
"There's a big ugly monster in my hole."

"Who are you?" said the little goat.

"I am the jackal who lives in this hole," said the jackal.

Now the little goat was very clever and when he heard that, he sang out,

"I am strong and
I am very brave.
I eat all the tigers
Who come to this cave!"

The jackal was even more afraid when he heard this.
He ran away as fast as his legs would carry him to tell his friend the tiger about the monster who was living in his hole in the ground.

"What is the matter?" asked the tiger when
he saw the jackal. "You have only just left me to
go home to your hole in the ground."

The jackal shook and shook with fear.

"There is a big ugly monster in my hole," he said.
"He says that he eats all tigers who go there."

"Oh does he?" roared the tiger. "He won't eat me!
Come along. I'll show you. I'll get him out
of your hole."

But the jackal was still very afraid.

"When the monster comes out of the hole, he will eat me," he said to the tiger. "You can run away, for your legs are long. I will be left alone with that terrible monster."

"No, no," said the tiger. "I won't leave you alone."

"I know what we can do," said the jackal. "Let me tie my tail to your tail. Then if you run away, I will be able to stay with you."

"Oh, very well," said the tiger. "Tie your tail to mine. Hurry up."

So the tiger and the jackal went back to the hole in the ground with their tails tied together.

The little goat heard them coming and
he was very, very afraid.
But he shouted out in a loud voice,
 "You fool, you fool,
 What have you done?
 I told you to bring me twenty tigers.
 You have tied up only one!"
 When the tiger heard this, he nearly
jumped out of his skin with fright.
The monster in the hole could eat twenty tigers!
How terrible he must be! How big and strong!
The jackal must have played a nasty trick on him.
He had tied him up by the tail to bring him to
the terrible monster in the hole.
What a fool he had been!

The tiger turned and ran for his life, pulling
the jackal along the ground behind him.
Every time the jackal bumped his head on
the ground he shouted out, but the tiger thought
it was the terrible monster chasing after him, so
he ran even faster.

The next day the little goat went home.
"Where have you been?" asked his mother.
"I have been chasing jackals,"
said the little goat. "And tigers!"

The wicked tiger

Once upon a time there was a wicked tiger.
He was kept in a cage in a village.
All day he tried to get out.

One day a kind old man came by.

"Good morning, sir," said the tiger.
"I can see you are a wise and kind old man.
Please will you help me?"

"Of course," said the kind old man.
"What can I do for you?"

"Please open the cage door for me," said the tiger.

"Very well," said the kind old man and he opened
the cage door.

The tiger jumped out of the cage.

"Now I am going to eat you up," he said.

"But that's not fair!" said the old man. "I helped you to get out of the cage and now you say you will eat me!"

"You were silly to let me out of the cage," said the wicked tiger. "You were not wise at all, so now I'm going to eat you up."

And the tiger got ready to jump on the old man.

"Wait!" said the old man. "You will be very wicked if you eat me. If you are kind and help someone, then they will always help you in return."

"That's not true," said the wicked tiger.

"Very well," said the kind old man. "Let us go and ask if what I have said is true or not."

The wicked tiger laughed. He knew that he would eat the old man anyway.

"All right," he said. "We will ask the river." So the wicked tiger and the kind old man went down to the river.

"River, river," said the tiger. "When you help people do they help you in return?"

"No, no," said the river. "I give people fresh clean water to drink and beautiful silver fish to eat. What do they do for me in return? They throw old bits of wood at me and throw all their rubbish in me as I go by."

"You see?" said the wicked tiger to the kind old man. "Now I will eat you up."

"Wait," said the kind old man. "Let us ask
that tree over there."

"Very well," said the wicked tiger.
"Tree, tree. When you help people do they
help you in return?"

"No, no," said the tree. "I give people
shade in the summer when the sun is
burning hot and I give them beautiful
fruit to eat.
What do they do for me in return?
They break my branches off and
cut names with knives in my bark."

18

"You see?" said the wicked tiger to the
kind old man. "Now I will eat you up."

"Wait," said the kind old man. "Here is a jackal.
Let us ask him, for jackals are very clever."

"Very well," said the wicked tiger.
"Tell me little jackal, when you help people
do they help you in return?"

Now the jackal was very clever.

"Why do you ask?" he said to the wicked tiger.

"Well," said the wicked tiger. "This old man let me out of my cage.
Now I am going to eat him up, but he says that if you are kind and help someone, then they will always help you in return."

"I see," said the jackal. "But first I must be sure that the old man was in a cage and that you let him out."

"No, no," said the wicked tiger.
"The old man wasn't in the cage.
I was in the cage. He let me out and
we went to the river . . ."

"Ah! I see," said the jackal. "The river was
in the cage and the old man let it out."

"No, no, no," shouted the wicked tiger.
"The river wasn't in the cage. Me! Me! Me!
I was in the cage. The old man let me out and
we went to the tree . . ."

"Ah! I see now," said the jackal. "The tree was
in the cage and the river let it out."

"No, no, no, you fool," shouted the wicked tiger.
"Come with me and I will show you what
happened."

So the wicked tiger, the kind old man and the clever jackal went back to the cage.

"Show me what happened,"
said the clever jackal.

"Listen to me," said the wicked tiger.
"I was inside the cage. I was very angry."

"Show me what you mean,"
said the clever jackal.

"You are a fool," said the tiger.
"You are not clever at all. I was in the cage like this . . ." and the tiger ran into the cage.

"I see," said the clever jackal.
"Now I understand at last."
And he quickly shut the door of
the cage and locked it.

The wicked tiger was very, very cross.
He knew that the clever jackal had tricked him.

"Let me out! Let me out!" he said.

The kind old man looked at the clever jackal and
the clever jackal looked at the kind old man.
They were both smiling.
But the tiger wasn't smiling at all.

The fox in the water

Once upon a time there was a little red fox.
One day he was very thirsty.
He went to the lake to have a drink.
He sat down by the lake and looked in the water.
Then he became very angry.
There was another fox in the water looking at him.
"Go away," said the Little Red Fox.
He looked as big as he could and he showed
all his teeth.

The fox in the water said nothing, but
showed all his teeth in return.

"Go away at once," said the Little Red Fox,
"or I will jump in the water and bite you,
you nasty ugly fox!"
But the fox in the water said nothing.

The Little Brown Duck heard the Little Red Fox.
"What is the matter?" she said.

"There's another fox in the water," said
the Little Red Fox. "I have told him to go away,
but he won't. I don't like him and he's very ugly."

"But . . . but that's not another fox,"
said the Little Brown Duck.

"Yes it is," shouted the Little Red Fox.
"I'm going to jump in the water and bite him!"

"I wouldn't do that," said the Little Brown Duck.

"Why not?" asked the Little Red Fox.
"I am thirsty, but I can't drink while that
nasty ugly fox is in the water. If I jump in
the water and bite him, he will go away."

"I'll tell you why not," said the
Little Brown Duck. "In the middle of the lake
is a terrible crocodile.
He will grab you and eat you for his dinner.
His teeth are like long white spears."

"Ho! Ho! I'm not afraid of a silly old
crocodile," said the Little Red Fox and
he jumped into the water.

The Little Red Fox swam round and round,
but he could not find the other fox at all.

"He's afraid of me. He must have gone to
the other side of the lake to get away from me,"
the Little Red Fox said to himself.
So he started to swim right across
the middle of the lake.
Then he heard a sound in the water
right behind him.
It was the terrible crocodile with the long teeth!
He was chasing the Little Red Fox across the lake!

"Oh dear!" said the Little Red Fox.
"I have been very silly. Why did I not listen to
the Little Brown Duck? That other fox wasn't
ugly at all. He was just as beautiful as me!"
    The Little Red Fox swam faster and faster across
the lake and the terrible crocodile swam after him.

At last the Little Red Fox reached
the other side of the lake.
He climbed out just in time and sat
on the bank, huffing and puffing.

"Now I am safe," he said. "That terrible crocodile
can't eat me for his dinner now."

But the Little Red Fox had left his tail
hanging down in the water . . .

Suddenly he felt a tug on the end of his tail.
He was being pulled back into the water!

"Help! Help!" he cried. "The terrible crocodile
has caught me and will eat me for his dinner!
Please, please help me!"

Suddenly the terrible crocodile let go
of his tail and the Little Red Fox was free.
He climbed back up the bank and this time
he made sure his tail was not hanging in the water.

"Why did the terrible crocodile let go
of my tail?" he said out loud.

"I'll tell you," said the Little Brown Duck.
"I swam underneath him and tickled his tummy."

"Oh, thank you, little friend," said the
Little Red Fox. "Next time I'll listen to you and
I won't do anything silly like that again.
And as for that other fox, why, I think
he is not really nasty and ugly.
He is really just as beautiful as me."

"Of course he is," said the Little Brown Duck.
"Of course he is!"